This book is presented to

_____

With love from

_____

Date

_____

The BLESSING

of a GRANDMOTHER'S LOVE

IDEALS PUBLICATIONS • NASHVILLE, TENNESSEE

ISBN 0-8249-5892-6

Published by Ideals Publications
535 Metroplex Drive, Suite 250, Nashville, Tennessee 37211
www.idealsbooks.com

Printed and bound in Italy

Compiled and edited by Peggy Schaefer, Melinda Rathjen
Designed by Marisa Calvin
Cover photograph by Comstock

1 3 5 7 9 10 8 6 4 2

ACKNOWLEDGMENTS

BENEDICT, ARLENE. From *Grandmothers.* Ariel Books, Andrews McMeel publisher, 1996. CAPPERS MAGAZINE. From
"A Date With Grandma," Sept. 4, 2001. Ogden Publishing. McREYNOLDS, FRIEDA. Verse from *Grandmothers Are
Like Snowflakes,* compiled by Janet Lanese, 1996. Published by Doubleday. REGIER, DeMAR. From *Gifts From Our
Grandmothers,* edited by Carol Dovi. Crown Publishing, Random House, 2000. ROGERS, STEPHEN D. From
"Thanks." Used by permission of the author. VIORST, JUDITH. "The Blissful Couple" from *Suddenly Sixty and Other
Shocks of Later Life.* Copyright © 2000 by the author. Simon & Schuster. Used by permission of Lescher & Lescher
Ltd. WYSE, LOIS. From *Funny, You Don't Look Like a Grandmother.* Copyright © 1989 by Lois Wyse. Used by permis-
sion of Crown Publishers, a division of Random House, Inc. Our sincere thanks to those authors or their heirs
who submitted material for use by Ideals Publications.

Every effort has been made to establish ownership and use of each selection in this book. The publisher will be
pleased to rectify any inadvertent errors or omissions in subsequent editions.

Photography Credits: Pages 13, 14–15, 24–25, 36–37, 38, 40–41, 44, 46–47, 50–51, age fotostock/SuperStock;
page 16, Rick Gomez/Masterfile; page 19, Russell Monk/Masterfile; pages 20–21, Tim Gartside/Alamy; page 23,
SuperStock; page 28, ImageState/Alamy; pages 30–31, G. Ahrens/SuperStock; page 43, Visions of America/Alamy;
page 52, Stock Connection Distribution/Alamy; page 57, Beateworks Inc./Alamy; page 60, Maria Mosolova/Alamy.

GRANDMOTHERS ARE
VOICES OF THE
PAST AND ROLE MODELS
OF THE PRESENT.
GRANDMOTHERS OPEN
THE DOORS TO THE FUTURE.
—HELEN KETCHUM

A GRANDMOTHER'S
LOVE . . .

delights

Grandma always made you feel she had been waiting to see just you all day and now the day was complete.

—Marcy DeMaree

Grandmothers are the people who take delight in hearing babies breathing into the telephone.

—Author Unknown

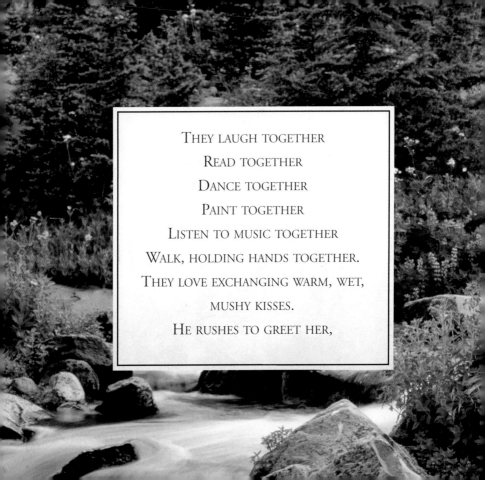

THEY LAUGH TOGETHER
READ TOGETHER
DANCE TOGETHER
PAINT TOGETHER
LISTEN TO MUSIC TOGETHER
WALK, HOLDING HANDS TOGETHER.
THEY LOVE EXCHANGING WARM, WET,
MUSHY KISSES.
HE RUSHES TO GREET HER,

His arms outstretched,
Joyfully calling her name
When he sees her arrive.
Who, you are wondering,
Is this blissful couple?
She is his grandma
He is almost five.
—Judith Viorst

*Grandmas hold our tiny hands for just a little while,
but our hearts forever.*

—AUTHOR UNKNOWN

*Grandmothers are all the wonderful things
The mind will never outgrow.*

—JUNE MASTERS BACHER

Thanks

Stephen D. Rogers

Few things thrill this man more than the sight of my grandmother's handwriting on an envelope. I always save that piece of mail for last, for when I am free to pay it the attention it deserves.

My grandmother buys discounted cards for their pictures and not the printed text, which in this case congratulates me on a new job. The words that matter are the ones she writes herself.

She starts where most people merely sign their name. She completely fills that page with her neat script, moves over to the facing page, and then finishes her note as the space runs out on the back of the card.

She is thanking me for hosting a birthday party. She doesn't simply say, "Thanks," which would still be more than I received from others. My grandmother describes every detail she appreciated, mentions the news she heard, and repeats the jokes that made her laugh. She recalls past parties I've thrown and dwells on the highlights.

Those who say that letter writing is a lost art never received mail from my grandmother, who has once again brightened my day and lessened my load.

A GRANDMOTHER'S
LOVE . . .

nurtures

Grandmas never run out of hugs or cookies.

—Author Unknown

*My grandmother remembers with her heart
those tender little childhood moments
that I have long forgotten.*

—Joyce K. Allen Logan

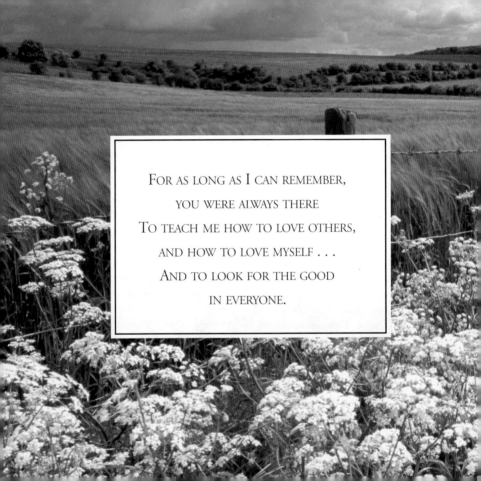

For as long as I can remember,
you were always there
To teach me how to love others,
and how to love myself . . .
And to look for the good
in everyone.

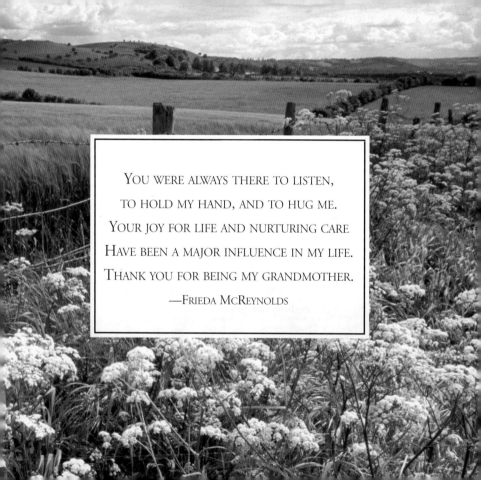

You were always there to listen,
to hold my hand, and to hug me.
Your joy for life and nurturing care
Have been a major influence in my life.
Thank you for being my grandmother.
—FRIEDA McREYNOLDS

MY GRANDMOTHER'S GARDEN

Carol Bessent Hayman

It has never surprised me that, wherever I lived, I always had a garden. The urge was deep inside me, twined around memories of my grandmother. Even her name, Rose, evokes images of a garden.

In my mind I can see her patiently watering her blooming yard, tending her geraniums and begonias, coaxing her old-fashioned yellow rose on our backyard trellis, and accepting compliments on her fragrant gardenias. Watching her, I learned to love the land. As the oldest grandchild, I became her helper, her errand girl, and almost her shadow. Today I live on the piece of land she knew and cultivated, in the house she dreamed of long before my grandfather built it for her. I am part of the town where she was born, married, and lived her life. Familiar things, shared thoughts, and warm memories surround me, and nowhere more than in my yard and garden.

Evenings often find me quietly enjoying the sights and scents of my garden, where I remember moonlit nights when I sat with my grandmother on the porch overlooking the yard and rocked to the rhythm of those dear surroundings. We spoke love's language, which is to read each other's thoughts and answer with soft words such as "Of course," "Always," and "Yes, tomorrow."

At evening, as shadows fall, I can see her among the flower beds, and I understand the words, "Welcome to my garden."

A grandmother is a little bit parent, a little bit teacher, and a little bit best friend.

—Author Unknown

Being grandparents sufficiently removes us from the responsibilities so that we can be friends.

—Allan Fromme

A GRANDMOTHER'S
LOVE . . .

accepts

A DATE WITH GRANDMA

From CAPPER'S magazine

We came from a big family, and our funds were limited. Eating out was an event that happened only on special occasions. The day of my first communion was to be my first meal out with Mom and Dad. I had watched with interest as this happened with my three older siblings.

Counting down the days, I was anxious—not just for the event, but for the exclusive lunch with my parents. I was disappointed when my big day arrived, and the tradition was broken. I wouldn't be going out. Instead, Dad

was going to cook out in my honor. We had cookouts every weekend, and to me a cookout was a poor substitute.

I went to my room and sobbed into my pillow. I didn't take into consideration that my mother had given birth to my little sister just the week before. Being seven years old, I saw the world only as it related to me.

But there was someone watching my distress who cared that I was hurt. A few weeks later, my grandma announced that she was taking me out to eat. As I was jumping up and down, my grandma's eyes were dancing with joy. She had twenty grandchildren, and all of us lived within fifty miles of each other. Having exclusive time with Grandma was rare.

The date was set, which sent my mom to the sewing machine, working feverishly on a new dress for my date with Grandma. My heart swelled with pride as I put on my red and white polka-dot dress.

Since Grandma didn't drive, it was my first time to take a taxi. At the restaurant, Grandma proudly told the waitress that I was her grandchild and that this was my first time to eat out.

After all this time, I remember what I ate. I can still smell the cheeseburger and fries and taste the best lemon iced tea I ever had. I remember my grandma smiling at me, pleased that I was enjoying myself.

I don't remember what we talked about, but I knew I had a Grandma who understood the disappointment of a seven-year-old. She made a special memory that is still precious to me forty-one years later.

Grandmothers are wise and patient. They give others the benefit of the doubt and are quick to grant forgiveness and acceptance when blame and condemnation would seem a more natural response. Courage in hardship and grace in victory come naturally to them.

They know how to take the edge

off criticism with a funny story and often make themselves the butt of jokes to defuse tension. They also know when to be serious, earning the respect of the generations with their insight, tenacity, and wisdom.

—ARLENE F. BENEDICT

Grandmother-grandchild relationships are simple.
Grandmas are short on criticism and long on love.

—Author Unknown

We should all have one person who knows
how to bless us despite the evidence.
Grandmother was that person to me.

—Phyllis Theroux

A GRANDMOTHER'S
LOVE . . .

teaches

GRANDMA'S CELLAR DOOR

DeMar Regier

The worn, weather-beaten cellar door slanted in such a way that its top, about a foot high, made an ideal ledge on which Grandma and I could sit. We observed the barn across the road, the outlying fields dotted with farm animals, the graceful willows near the house, and the wide expanse of prairie sky that stretched in every direction. Like two birds perched on a low limb, Grandma and I talked about all the happenings around us or sat quietly, happy to be part of it all.

There, close to Grandma's side, listening to her observations and wise questions, I learned about life and the lessons that nature can teach. During harvest time, while we examined ripening kernels of wheat, I learned how important little seeds are; how women and men shared the work; that it takes time to grow.

And then there were Grandma's questions and comments. When she said, "That's a crimson sunset. There'll be no rain tomorrow." "It's so still. A storm is on the way." How did she know? Or when she asked, "Which stars would you like over your bed?" I pondered.

In time, the old cellar door was replaced by school doors, but nothing ever supplanted the heritage of Grandma's wisdom, wonder, and love of nature.

She taught me how to study things slowly, with care, how to detect and relish the beauty in all.

—Opal Palmer Adisa

A grandmother is a babysitter who watches the kids instead of the television.

—Author Unknown

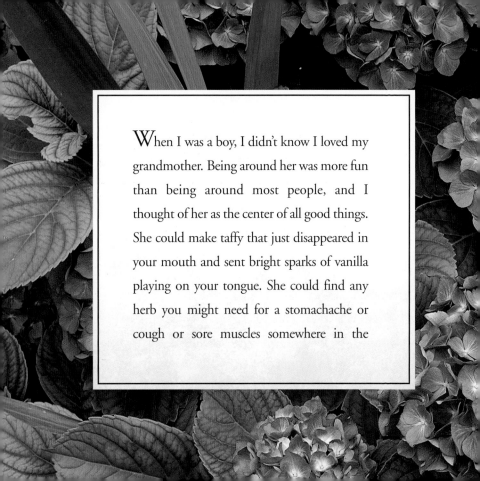

When I was a boy, I didn't know I loved my grandmother. Being around her was more fun than being around most people, and I thought of her as the center of all good things. She could make taffy that just disappeared in your mouth and sent bright sparks of vanilla playing on your tongue. She could find any herb you might need for a stomachache or cough or sore muscles somewhere in the woods near her farm. She could tell a better story than you might ever hear anywhere else, and she could understand me when I tried to sort out the confusing parts of life.

What lasts in recall of her is how she helped people—including me—put confusion to rest. She didn't lecture or explain how things ought to be; she just walked along beside me, and we looked at the world together.

—WALKER MEADE

Grandmothers are to life
what the PhD is to education.
There is nothing you can feel,
taste, expect, predict, or want
that the grandmothers in your family
do not know about in detail.

—LOIS WYSE

A GRANDMOTHER'S
LOVE . . .

comforts

What children need most
are the essentials that grandparents
provide in abundance.
They give unconditional love,
kindness, patience, humor,
comfort, lessons in life.
And, most importantly, cookies.

—RUDOLPH GIULIANI

I dream
Of a friendly tree with boughs outstretched
To welcome me home when my heart
     needs rest;
Of a flower-lined walk, smiling gay and sweet,
That beckons my step and gladdens my feet;

Of an open door round whose worn sill twines
The secret of peace in wisteria vines;

And the blessed vision of your dear face,

Grandmother-mine—by the fireplace.

I turn from striving that seemed worthwhile

To the sure serenity of your smile;

To your voice of love with enduring charms—

The end of the road is your sheltering arms.

—MEREDITH GRAY

GRANDMA'S LEGACY

Shannon Dyer

Warm and rich, it dribbles from the spoon. At once it is fragile and delicate, yet common and solid. The simplicity of my grandmother's butter sauce belies its magical taste. One spoonful holds the history of family tradition. I've got Grandma memories, like every child: I remember summers sitting on the front porch, running with my cousins through her big house, wearing the warm sweaters she'd knit. But mostly, those childhood memories of Grandma center around the kitchen.

It's the butter sauce that brings my grandmother to my

heart. It tastes like Grandma [is], all warm and sweet and uncomplicated. It might be her very essence. There's no trick, no secret, to making it. Dump everything in a pan, heat it, and stir. I've never ruined it. I don't think a person could. I stand at the stove and stir the mystical concoction, and when my girls aren't looking, I dip my fingers in and steal tastes, something so uncouth I'd never tolerate it from them. It isn't all about the taste, though everyone I've served it to loves it; it's about my grandma.

I am connected to Grandma, almost like I can feel her blood in my veins, and that of the noble line that stretches back for generations, full of strong women, pioneers, ground breakers, intelligent and assertive. I am proud to be carrying their genes, and sometimes I think they are walking with me, daring me to step up and claim my place in the world; I deserve it as a birthright. This pride in my heritage was handed down to me from my grandmother. I sat down on her living room floor one recent summer and helped her sort through a box of pictures, documents, and newspaper clippings. Suddenly the wise, calm woman who sits in her recliner in the avocado-green living room became a spirited young wife, and before that, a mischievous girl. She's a link in the chain, just like me. Grandma has been the keeper of the family for three generations. She guarded our history and gave me the gift and responsibility to carry on the continuity of the ages.

So I make the butter sauce and pour it over the basic apple cake. As I watch my little girls smack their lips over each golden spoonful, I pass along the torch, because my grandma's blood flows in their veins too, and that's a legacy to be proud of.

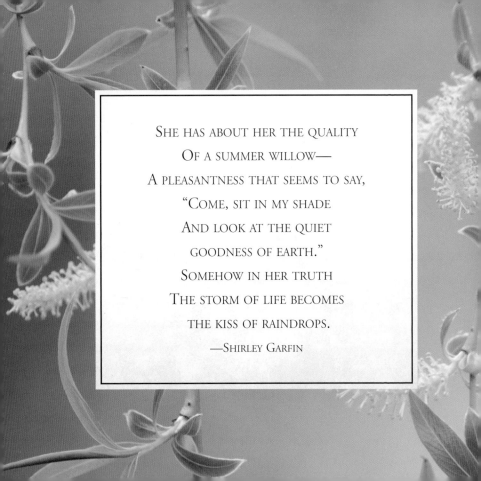

SHE HAS ABOUT HER THE QUALITY
OF A SUMMER WILLOW—
A PLEASANTNESS THAT SEEMS TO SAY,
"COME, SIT IN MY SHADE
AND LOOK AT THE QUIET
GOODNESS OF EARTH."
SOMEHOW IN HER TRUTH
THE STORM OF LIFE BECOMES
THE KISS OF RAINDROPS.
—SHIRLEY GARFIN